Table des matières

KT-115-951

Try to read the question and choose an answer on your own.

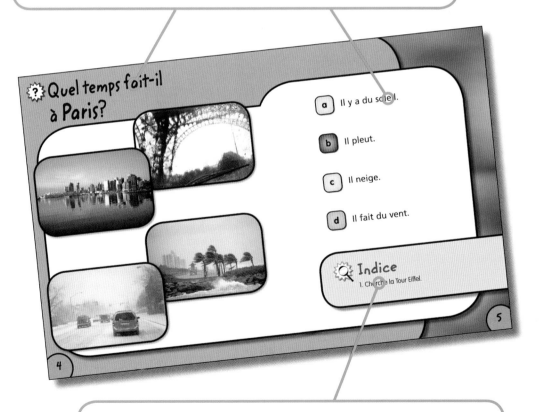

You might want some help with text like this.

? Quel temps fait-il à Paris?

Quel temps fait-il?

Fiona Undrill

Heinemann
LIBRARY

Weather

www.heinemann.co.uk/library
Visit our website to find out more information about Heinemann Library books.

To order:
☎ Phone 44 (0) 1865 888066
  Send a fax to 44 (0) 1865 314091
📄 Visit the Heinemann Bookshop at www.heinemann.co.uk/library to browse our
💻 catalogue and order online.

First published in Great Britain by Heinemann Library, Halley Court, Jordan Hill, Oxford OX2 8EJ, part of Harcourt Education. Heinemann is a registered trademark of Harcourt Education Ltd.

© Harcourt Education Ltd 2007

Editorial: Charlotte Guillain
Design: Joanna Hinton-Malivoire
Map illustration: International Mapping Associates
Picture research: Ruth Blair
Production: Duncan Gilbert

Printed and bound in China by Leo Paper Group.

ISBN 9780431931258 (hardback)
11 10 09 08 07
10 9 8 7 6 5 4 3 2 1
ISBN 9780431931357 (paperback)
11 10 09 08 07
10 9 8 7 6 5 4 3 2 1

British Library Cataloguing in Publication Data
Undrill, Fiona
Quel temps fait-il? : weather. - (Modern foreign languages readers)
1. French language - Readers - Weather 2. Weather - Juvenile literature 3. Vocabulary - Juvenile literature
448.6'421
A full catalogue record for this book is available from the British Library.

Acknowledgements
The publishers would like to thank the following for permission to reproduce photographs:
© Alamy pp. **16** top left (Oote Boe Photography), **16** top right (Greg Vaughn), **20** botom right (Andre Jenny); © Corbis pp. **3** top right, **4** top right (Bettmann), **3** bottom right, **4** bottom right (Warren Faidley), **8** bottom right, **12** bottom left (image100), **12** bottom right (Owen Franken), **16** bottom left (Tony Arruza); © Getty Images p. **20** top right (Photodisc); © istockphoto.com pp. **3** bottom left, **4** bottom left, **8** top left, **8** top right, **8** bottom left, **12** top right, **19** bottom, **20** top left, **23** bottom; © 2007 Jupiter Images Corporation pp. **3** top left, **4** top left, **7** bottom, **7** top, **10**, **12** top left, **15** bottom, **15** top, **16** bottom right, **19** top, **20** bottom left, **23** top

Cover photograph reproduced with permission of © Alamy (Jim Zuckerman).

Every effort has been made to contact copyright holders of any material reproduced in this book. Any omissions will be rectified in subsequent printings if notice is given to the publishers.

a Il y a du soleil.

b Il pleut.

c Il neige.

d Il fait du vent.

 **Indice**

1. Cherche la Tour Eiffel.

Réponse

b Il pleut.

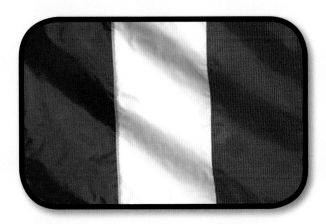

La France

Capitale: Paris

Population: 61 millions

Langue officielle: le français

La Tour Eiffel

Quel temps fait-il au Québec, Canada?

a	Il fait froid.
b	Il fait beau.
c	Il fait chaud.
d	Il y a des nuages.

 Indices

1. Cherche le drapeau rouge et blanc du Canada.
2. Dans l'image, il y a de la neige.

✓ Réponse

a Il fait froid.

Le Canada

Capitale: Ottowa

Population: 33 millions

Langues officielles: l'anglais, le français

LE CANADA

Vancouver

Québec

Ottawa

New York

LES ETATS-UNIS

Chicago

Washington DC

Los Angeles

Mexico

❓ Quel temps fait-il à Londres?

a Il fait froid.

b Il fait beau.

c Il y a des nuages.

d Il pleut.

 Indices

1. Cherche Big Ben.
2. Il y a une rivière à Londres.

Réponse

b Il fait beau.

Le Royaume-Uni

Capitale: Londres

Population: 61 millions

Langue officielle: l'anglais

Big Ben

Quel temps fait-il à New York?

a Il y a du brouillard.

b Il fait beau.

c Il fait du vent.

d Il fait chaud.

 Indice

1. Cherche la Statue de la Liberté.

Réponse

a Il y a du brouillard.

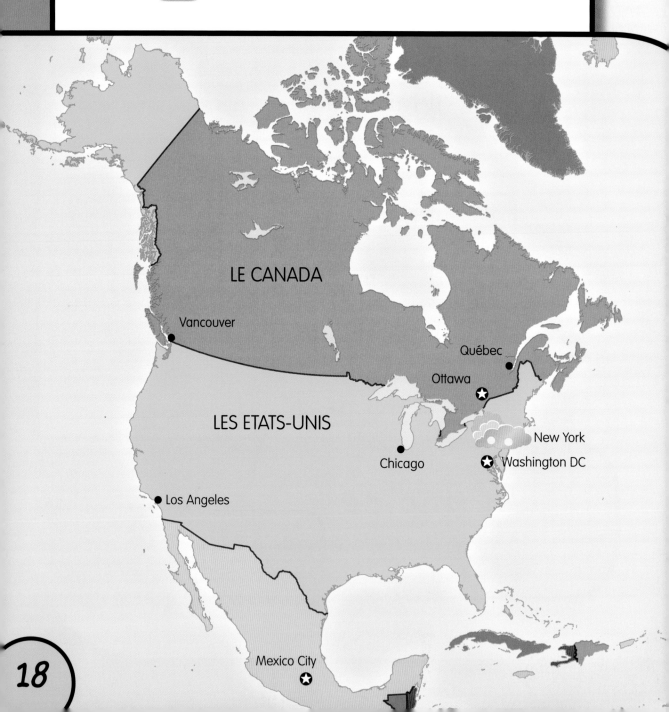

LE CANADA

Vancouver

Québec

Ottawa

LES ETATS-UNIS

New York

Chicago

Washington DC

Los Angeles

Mexico City

Les États-Unis

Capitale: Washington DC

Population: 299 millions

Langue officielle: l'anglais

La Statue de la Liberté

Quel temps fait-il dans les Alpes Suisses?

a Il neige.

b Il y a du brouillard.

c Il fait chaud.

d Il y a du soleil.

 Indices

1. Cherche le drapeau rouge et blanc de la Suisse.
2. Les Alpes sont des montagnes.

d Il y a du soleil.

La Suisse

Capitale: Genève

Population: 8 millions

Langues officielles:

- l'allemand
- le français
- l'italien
- le romanche

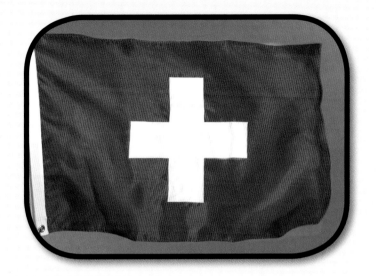

Le chocolat suisse

Vocabulaire

Français Anglais page

l'allemand German (language) 23
les Alpes the Alps 21
les Alpes Suisses the Swiss Alps 21
l'anglais English (language) 10, 15, 19
blanc white 9, 21
la capitale capital city 7, 10, 15, 19, 23
le Canada Canada 8, 9, 10
une casse tête puzzle 3
chercher to look for 5, 9, 13, 17, 21
le chocolat chocolate 23
dans in 9, 20
un drapeau flag 9, 21
et and 9, 21
les Etats-Unis the United States of America 19
le français French (language) 7, 10, 23
la France France 7
Il fait beau. It's fine weather. 9, 13, 14, 17
Il fait chaud. It's hot. 9, 17, 21
Il fait du vent. It's windy. 5, 17
Il fait froid. It's cold. 9, 10, 13
Il neige. It's snowing. 5, 21
Il pleut. It's raining. 5, 13
Il y a des nuages. It's cloudy. 9, 13
Il y a du brouillard. It's foggy. 17, 18, 21
Il y a du soleil. It's sunny. 5, 21, 23
une image picture 9
un indice clue 5, 9, 13, 17, 21
l'italien Italian (language) 23

la langue officielle official language 7, 10, 15, 19, 23
Londres London 12, 13
une montagne mountain 21
la neige snow 9
la population population 7, 10, 15, 19, 23
le romanche Romansh 23
Quel temps fait-il? What's the weather like? 1, 4, 8, 12, 16, 20
une réponse answer 6, 10, 14, 18, 22
une rivière river 13
rouge red 9, 21
le Royaume-Uni the United Kingdom 15
la Statue de la Liberté the Statue of Liberty 17, 19
la Suisse Switzerland 21, 23
suisse Swiss 20, 23
la table des matières contents 3
la Tour Eiffel the Eiffel tower 5, 7
le vocabulaire vocabulary 3, 24